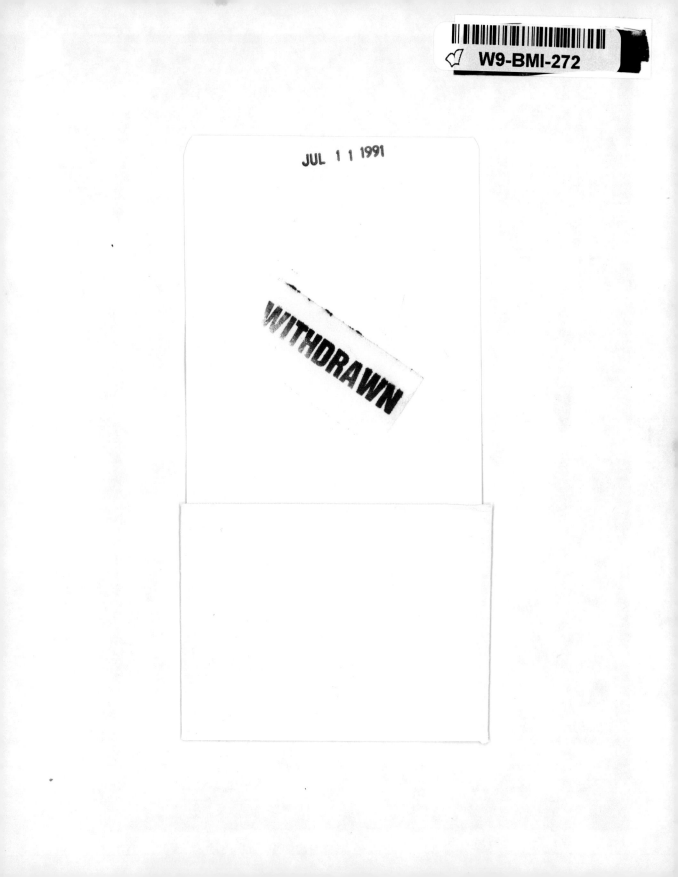

Children of the World

Costa Rica

For a free color catalog describing Gareth Stevens' list of high-quality children's books, call 1-800-341-3569 (USA) or 1-800-461-9120 (Canada).

For their help in the preparation of *Children of the World: Costa Rica*, the writer and editors gratefully thank the Friends (Quaker) Peace Center in San José, Costa Rica; Professor Michael Fleet, Marquette University, Milwaukee; Professor Howard Handelman, University of Wisconsin-Milwaukee; and Professor Cecilia Rodriguez, University of Wisconsin-Waukesha.

Flag illustration on page 48, © Flag Research Center.

Library of Congress Cataloging-in-Publication Data

Cummins, Ronnie.
    Costa Rica / written by Ronald Cummins ; photography by Rose Welch.
        p. cm. — (Children of the world)
      Summary: Presents the life of an eleven-year-old girl and her family in Costa Rica, describing her home and school activities and discussing the history, geography, ethnic composition, natural resources, languages, government, religions, culture, and economics of her country.
    ISBN 0-8368-0222-5
    1. Costa Rica—Social life and customs—Juvenile literature. 2. Children—Costa Rica—Juvenile literature. [1. Family life—Costa Rica. 2. Costa Rica.] I. Welch, Rose, ill. II. Title. III. Series: Children of the world (Milwaukee, Wis.)
F1543.8.C86   1990
972.86—dc20   89-43138

A Gareth Stevens Children's Books edition

Edited, designed, and produced by
Gareth Stevens Children's Books
RiverCenter Building, Suite 201
1555 North RiverCenter Drive
Milwaukee, Wisconsin 53212, USA

Series editor: Valerie Weber
Editor: Amy Bauman
Research editor: Kathleen Weisfeld Barrilleaux
Layout: Kate Kriege
Map design: Sheri Gibbs

Printed in the United States of America

1 2 3 4 5 6 7 8 9 96 95 94 93 92 91 90

Children of the World
Costa Rica

Text by Ronnie Cummins
Photography by Rose Welch

Gareth Stevens Children's Books
MILWAUKEE

. . . a note about *Children of the World*:

The children of the world live in fishing towns, Arctic regions, and urban centers, on islands and in mountain valleys, on sheep ranches and fruit farms. This series follows one child in each country through the pattern of his or her life. Candid photographs show the children with their families, at school, at play, and in their communities. The text describes the dreams of the children and, often through their own words, tells how they see themselves and their lives.

Each book also explores events that are unique to the country in which the child lives, including festivals, religious ceremonies, and national holidays. The *Children of the World* series does more than tell about foreign countries. It introduces the children of each country and shows readers what it is like to be a child in that country.

Children of the World includes the following published and soon-to-be-published titles:

. . . and about *Costa Rica*:

Eleven-year-old Cristiana lives in a mountain village, where she works on her family's small dairy farm and in their modest restaurant. She plans to study agriculture in college. Meanwhile, she's happy to ride her horse along mountain trails.

To enhance this book's value in libraries and classrooms, comprehensive reference sections include up-to-date information about Costa Rica's geography, demographics, language, currency, education, culture, industry, and natural resources. *Costa Rica* also features a bibliography, research topics, activity projects, and discussions of such subjects as San José, the country's history, political system, and ethnic and religious composition.

The living conditions and experiences of children in Costa Rica may vary, but all enjoy a high standard of living and broad educational opportunities. The reference sections help bring to life for young readers the uniqueness of Costa Rica's development. Of particular interest are discussions of Costa Rica's disbandment of its army, its unusually stable government, and its commitment to peace among its Central American neighbors.

CONTENTS

LIVING IN COSTA RICA:
Cristiana, a Farm Girl from the Mountains

Eleven-year-old Evelyn Cristiana Gonzáles-Hidalgo lives on a farm in the mountain village of Sacramento, Costa Rica. Cristiana and her family live in a wooden house overlooking the slopes of Barva, one of Costa Rica's tallest volcanoes. Cristiana's family includes her parents, Obdulio and Ana Beliza; her brother, Uriel; and her sister, Olga Patricia. Olga, who is 15, attends high school in Heredia, a town in the valley below Sacramento.

The small village of Sacramento usually doesn't show on maps of Costa Rica. Cristiana says she is glad to live in this friendly community. All of the several hundred residents know one another and many are related. Cristiana is surrounded by her grandparents and many uncles, aunts, and cousins. Their houses and farms are scattered all throughout the area.

Opposite: In a rare quiet moment, the Gonzáles-Hidalgo family gathers outside their mountain home in Sacramento. With Cristiana are her parents, Obdulio and Ana Beliza, and her brother, Uriel. Olga, Cristiana's older sister, is away at school. ▶

The family never tires of the view from their Sacramento home. At 7,000 feet (2,100 m) above sea level, Sacramento lies above both Heredia and San José on the slopes of Barva Volcano. At this height, much of the mountain stretches out below the small farming village.

Obdulio works as a carpenter for a hotel near Sacramento when he's not working on the family farm or in the restaurant.

Cristiana's Home and Family Farm

Cristiana and her family live on a small dairy farm. In addition to caring for the cows, chickens, and horses, they also tend a garden in which they grow most of their own vegetables and fruits. And if that isn't enough to keep everyone busy, the family also runs a restaurant, which is attached to the house. There, Cristiana's parents serve delicious homemade dishes to both tourists and local people.

Cristiana's father, Obdulio, is a skilled carpenter. He built the family's five-room house with the help of relatives and friends. Traditionally, relatives, friends, and neighbors pitch in whenever a family builds a house or barn. They cut the lumber from neighboring forests and do the work by hand without the use of electrical tools.

Ana Beliza manages the family restaurant, although everyone helps out.

Now that he is 14, Uriel handles many of the farm tasks.

Cristiana helps out at home, on the farm, in the restaurant, or wherever she can.

11

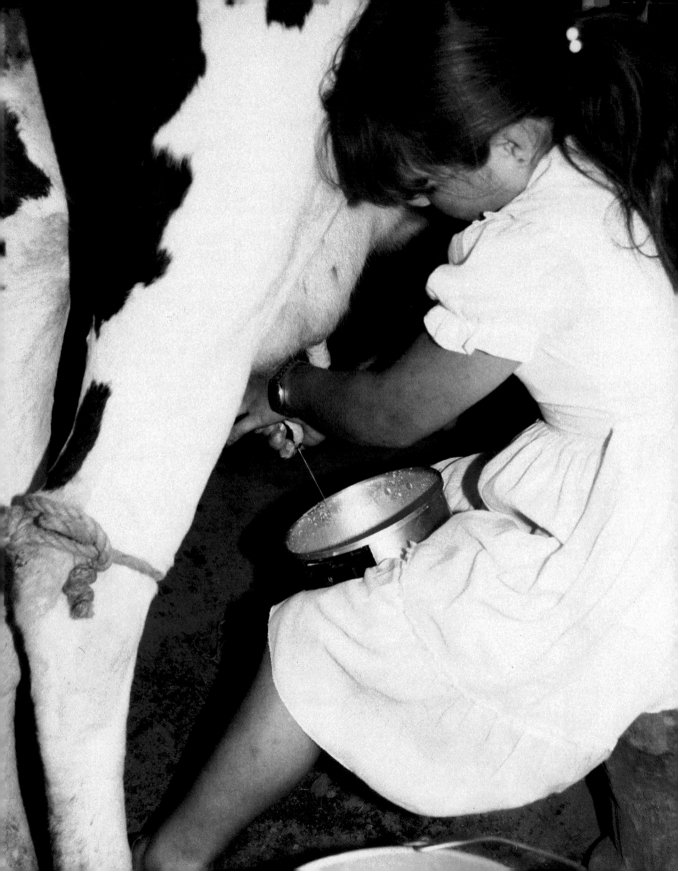

A Typical Morning for the Sacramento Farm Girl

Cristiana's day begins at 5:30 a.m. She wakes, dresses, and hurries to the pasture to bring the cows in for milking. Although it's barely light outside, this is one of Cristiana's favorite times of day. The birds sing from trees against the colorful sunrise sky, and the air feels fresh and cool. Peacefulness fills Cristiana as she tends to the four dairy cows. In the barn, after securing the cows in their harnesses, she feeds and washes them. Finally, sitting on a low wooden stool, she milks each cow by hand.

After milking them, Cristiana leads the cows back out to the pasture. Walking back to the house, she remembers learning to milk the cows when she was just seven years old. She can now milk a cow as well as most adults. Smiling to herself, she carries the stainless steel pail full of fresh milk into the house.

◀ Opposite: It takes strong hands to milk the cows.

Left: Carrying a pail of fresh milk, Cristiana heads back toward the house where she knows that breakfast will be waiting.
Below: Before leaving for school, Cristiana leads the cows back to the pasture where they graze all day.

13

Fresh tomatoes from the garden add color to Cristiana's waiting breakfast.

By 6:30, Cristiana sits down to breakfast, which usually consists of rice, black beans, fried *plátanos* (a type of banana), and *café con leche* (coffee with milk). A hot breakfast tastes good after she has been working outside in the chilly morning air.

After breakfast, Cristiana finishes her chores. School doesn't begin until 11:00 a.m., so she has plenty of time. She begins by splitting wood, which is one of her favorite chores. Although she is small, Cristiana is quite strong, so she swings her axe with no trouble. Sometimes Uriel helps her, and they have a contest to see who can split the most wood in five minutes. As usual, Cristiana splits enough wood to last the whole day. Like everyone else in the village, the family cooks and heats with a wood stove. Even though it never snows in Sacramento, it gets quite cool at night and in the early mornings. Without the stove's heat on those frosty mornings, Cristiana knows she'd never get out of bed.

Left and opposite: Cristiana pulls wood from a woodpile for splitting. Then, using an axe that is almost taller than she is, she splits the wood into pieces small enough to fit into the stove. ▶

After splitting firewood, Cristiana feeds the chickens and the geese, calling them with a clucking sound as she throws out kernels of corn.   Finally, Cristiana feeds her favorite animal — her puppy, Caballito. Caballito, whose name is Spanish for "little horse," gets a bowl of milk and some stale bread. By the time Cristiana has finished feeding the animals, it's nine o'clock.

Cristiana thinks feeding the turkeys, geese, and chickens is more fun than work. But just in case an especially hungry bird should mistake her toes for kernels of corn, Cristiana keeps her distance.

Preparing for school, Cristiana shines her shoes and puts on her uniform — a blue skirt and a white shirt — similar to that worn by most Costa Rican schoolgirls. Cristiana doesn't mind wearing a uniform; she is used to it. School rules require the students to wear uniforms, and Cristiana can't imagine dressing any other way. In addition, her parents say that if schools didn't require uniforms, many families would not be able to afford school clothes for their children.

Since Caballito eats so quickly, Cristiana always has time to play with him before school.

Cristiana works at putting a shine on her school shoes.

Having her hair brushed out is one of the most relaxing chores of the morning.

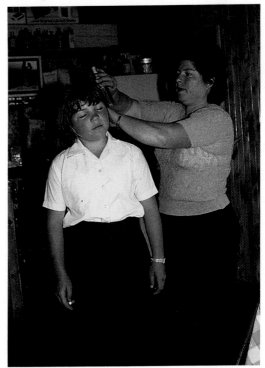

17

Cristiana's Elementary School

Cristiana has only a short walk from her house to the school, but it's a steep climb up the mountain road. Green pastures and a soccer field surround the two-room schoolhouse, Escuela Lourdes, which has only 30 students and one teacher. Over the years, the small school has earned a reputation for its excellent teachers.

Cristiana and the other children go to school for nine months a year and have a long vacation in November and December. In her elementary school, grades one through three attend classes in the morning, while grades four through six attend classes from 11:00 a.m. until 3:00 p.m. Cristiana's fourth- and fifth-grade class has three boys and eight girls, including her friend, Liliana, who is also 11 years old. Together the girls study history, reading, writing, geography, math, science, and art. Cristiana hopes someday to attend college, where she'd like to study agriculture.

◀ Opposite: Cristiana knows all the shortcuts to school through neighboring pastures and across streambeds.
Below: Cristiana, Liliana (farthest right), and their classmates pose with their teacher, Melvin Chavéz, outside of the schoolhouse, Escuela Lourdes.

For junior and senior high school, Sacramento students must travel to Heredia. This means a 30-minute walk to the bus stop each morning and then an hour's ride on the bus. People in Sacramento don't travel much and think this is a long trip. To avoid it, some students, like Olga, live with relatives in Heredia and return home only on weekends. If Olga goes on to college, she will go to school either in Heredia or in San José, which is even farther.

Today, Cristiana's teacher, *Don* Melvin, gives a lesson about the rain forest. (In Spanish, use of the title *Don* or *Doña* before a first name is a sign of respect.) He tells the students how important it is for Costa Rica and other countries to preserve their remaining rain forests, because they help protect a vital layer of Earth's atmosphere, called the ozone layer. The ozone shields Earth from the sun's harmful ultraviolet rays. As part of their studies, Don Melvin has scheduled a class trip to a nearby rain forest. The forest fascinates Cristiana, so she looks forward to the class trip.

Cristiana can't wait until she is old enough to go to school in Heredia, just as her sister, Olga, does.

Above: Cristiana displays her textbooks and notebooks against her book bag.

Right: During a geography lesson, some of Cristiana's classmates refer to the globe to locate the areas where rain forests grow.

Cristiana and her classmates crowd around Don Melvin as he gives a lecture on Costa Rica's dwindling rain forests.

At recess, the students play their favorite games of *policía y ladrónes* (cops and robbers), and hide-and-seek. Then, just before classes start again, the children eat a snack prepared by Doña Teresita, who owns the restaurant across the street from the school. Usually the snack consists of a fresh fruit drink and a corn tortilla filled with cheese and sausage.

Left: The many bushes and trees surrounding the school offer ample hiding places for a good game of hide-and-seek.
Below: Recess allows Cristiana and her classmates the chance to vent their energies.

Above: After particularly rough play at recess, Cristiana and her friend Liliana wash up before going back to class.
Below: Before class starts again, the children devour their midday snack.

Compared to other Latin American countries, Costa Rica spends a large percentage of its budget on education. The government can afford this, in part, because the constitution of 1948 abolished the country's army. Headed by José Figueres Ferrer, the government saw this as a way to bring peace to Costa Rica. Today, Costa Rica spends very little on weapons or defense. The money this saves goes toward education and other social services. When Cristiana reads about wars being fought all over the world, she is proud that her country abolished its army.

Below: Although Doña Teresita prepares the snack, the children clean up afterward.

Cristiana Visits the Farm

Cristiana often visits her grandparents on their farm. One of her favorite things about the farm is the large, colorful flower garden that her great-grandmother planted years ago. Cristiana and her grandmother often stroll among the flowers, looking for new blooms. Cristiana cuts some to take home. Winding through the garden, Cristiana imagines her great-grandmother walking the same paths.

Cristiana and her grandmother spend a lot of time walking and talking in the garden that surrounds the house.

Cristiana cuts fresh flowers to decorate the restaurant.

On weekends, Cristiana helps her grandparents milk their cows. They milk the 20 cows by hand, so it's quite a difficult task. During the week, Cristiana's father and her Uncle Martin help her grandfather do the milking. They then run the milk through an electrically powered cooler, which helps prevent the growth of harmful bacteria. Later, they strain the milk and pour it into sterilized steel containers. Cristiana's grandmother saves some of the milk to make cheese and sour cream.

Below: Uncle Martin patiently strains the cooled milk through the cheesecloth.

Cristiana leads Pajarito down the road to meet the milkman.

As part of her chores, Cristiana delivers the fresh milk to the milkman. She doesn't mind this task, because it means spending time with the family's horse, Pajarito. With the help of her brother, Cristiana straps the milk containers onto Pajarito's back and leads him about a half mile (1 km) down the road. There, she waits for the milkman, who loads the containers into his truck and takes them down into the valley, where he delivers the milk door to door.

The milkman exchanges empty milk containers for the full ones Cristiana brings him.

A plate of her grandmother's pastries tempts Cristiana.

Uncle Martin joins Cristiana for something to eat. After a morning of hard work, everything tastes especially good.

By the time Cristiana returns to the house, it's time for a break. Everyone piles into the kitchen, where her grandmother has prepared a meal of bread, fresh cheese, and homemade pastries. Coffee brews on the stove, too. As Cristiana breathes in its rich scent, she understands why Costa Rica is famous for its coffee. When she has eaten her fill, Cristiana turns on the radio. Leaning back, she takes a moment to relax and listen to the music. Many of her favorite songs are in English and were recorded in the United States. She wonders if the songs are still popular there.

Cristiana tunes in a station, hoping to find some of her favorite songs.

A colorful sign calls passing travelers into La Campesina.

Ana Beliza attends to food cooking on the huge stove that serves the restaurant.

La Campesina, the Gonzáles-Hidalgo Family Restaurant

Obdulio built the family restaurant a year ago. Called *La Campesina*, Spanish for "the country woman," it is popular with both local people and tourists. Over the wood stove in the kitchen, Cristiana's parents prepare the food — much of which is produced on the Gonzáles farm. Specialties include hearty soups, shish kebabs, *flan de coco* (coconut custard), and fresh sour cream and tortillas.

The family works together to run the restaurant and to keep up with the milking, the garden, and the other chores. Cristiana often helps out in the kitchen and has learned many of her mother's cooking skills. At times when she's working, Cristiana wishes she could be outside riding her horse or playing with her friends. Her mother understands this and sometimes tells Cristiana to go and play even before the work is finished.

During the week, the Gonzáles family serves only a few customers. But on Saturdays and Sundays, people suddenly crowd the restaurant. When that happens, Cristiana's mother, father, and aunt all work in the kitchen.

Above: The restaurant menu hangs where everyone can see it. Part of Cristiana's job is to keep the menu updated. Because Obdulio often makes fresh desserts, the menu items change almost daily.
Right: While everyone else is busy in the kitchen, Cristiana keeps the dining area clean.

Many of the restaurant customers are people passing through Sacramento on weekend visits to Braulio Carrillo National Park. This park — one of Costa Rica's many national parks — is located just 2.5 miles (4 km) up the road. But Cristiana thinks that many people come just for the view of Costa Rica's Central Valley from the back of their restaurant. At night, thousands of lights twinkle in San José below them. Although Cristiana and her family have lived on the mountain all their lives, they never tire of its beauty.

Below: The colorful lights of San José flood the valley below Sacramento. Cristiana and her family also take pleasure in the view and know that many of their customers do, too.

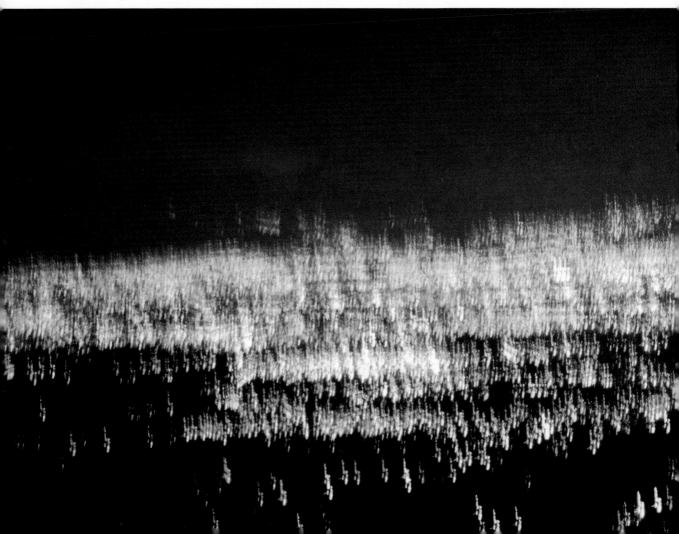

Cristiana's father is building an outdoor patio so that their customers can sit outside and enjoy the magnificent view. As he measures and cuts the lumber or pounds nails, he explains each step to Cristiana and Uriel. Cristiana listens to his every word, and she notices that Uriel listens just as eagerly. Working with her father makes Cristiana feel close to him.

Right: During a slow time at the restaurant, Obdulio turns his attention to the outdoor patio.

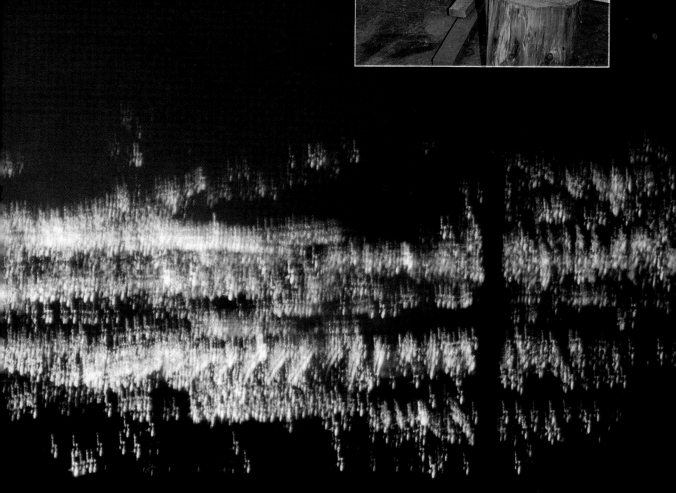

Free Time for Cristiana

When she has a little free time, Cristiana usually goes looking for her friends Liliana and Maria. Some days, the girls walk to Cristiana's family farm. If they don't have much time, they walk only as far as the store near their school. The store, which is owned by Doña Teresita, serves as a local gathering place. The children can usually find something to do there.

Uriel saddles Pajarito for Cristiana.

◀ Opposite: It won't be long until Cristiana's feet reach the stirrups.
Below: Cristiana's trip to the potato patch proves worth the ride.

Cristiana spends some afternoons riding Pajarito. After Uriel finishes milking cows at his grandparents' farm, he brings the horse back with him to the house. With his help, Cristiana then saddles Pajarito for a ride. Today, Cristiana's mother has asked her to ride out to the potato patch on her grandparents' farm to see if any of the potatoes are ready to harvest. Cristiana gallops away down the road, wishing that she didn't have school or chores to worry about so she could ride Pajarito all day.

Cristiana spends some of her afternoons alone reading, watching television, and doing her homework. On these days, she waits for her father to finish his work and then asks him to take her for a ride on his motorcycle. Cristiana thinks there's nothing like riding up and down the mountain roads on a motorcycle. As the wind rushes at them, she holds tightly to her father.

Obdulio revs the motorcycle's engine as he and Cristiana get ready for a spin up the mountain. The turns make Cristiana's heart pound.

Not all of Cristiana's afternoons are as hair-raising. Here she curls up with the many dolls and toys that share her bed.

When Olga is away from home, Cristiana has their bedroom all to herself. Although she misses her sister very much, having her own room makes Cristiana feel grown-up.

Today, without being asked, Cristiana straightens her bedroom. She carefully arranges her dolls and stuffed animals on her bed. They keep her company until Olga comes home from Heredia on the weekends. All week long, Cristiana looks forward to seeing Olga and hearing stories about what's been happening in Heredia. With a population of 30,000, that city is quite different from Sacramento. Heredia entices Cristiana with its shops, movie theaters, and large public swimming pool. In three years, she will attend the junior high school there, and she can hardly wait.

A typical breakfast consists of corn tortillas, a bowl of fresh sour cream, and café con leche.

Her mother's shish kebabs make Cristiana hungry any time of day.

Obdulio's flan de coco has given the restaurant a reputation for having mouth-watering desserts.

Heredia's tropical fruit stands attract many buyers. Many of the fruits offered, such as bananas and pineapples, are grown farther down the slopes of Barva.

The Market and Typical Foods of Heredia

Because the small village store can't carry everything that the people need, the family travels to Heredia's market for certain items. The city is a long bus ride away, but Cristiana gladly seizes the chance to go. Once there, she and Uriel ignore the vendors selling potatoes, carrots, squash, and beans; these they can find in Sacramento. Instead, they browse among the tropical fruits, such as bananas and pineapples, which are grown on the lower slopes of the mountains and along the coasts.

Traditional Costa Rican foods include tortillas, rice, beans, potatoes, eggs, and fruit. The family chooses their breakfast and lunch from these. In the evening, Ana Beliza serves a meat or cheese dish with a fresh salad. Sometimes, a fresh dessert tops off the meal. When Obdulio makes desserts for the restaurant, he makes extra for the family. Tonight they're eating flan de coco.

Before Mass, Cristiana arranges flowers from her grandmother's garden around the church altar.

Sunday Church Services in Sacramento

Cristiana looks forward to Sundays, when life seems to run a little slower than it does the rest of the week. Sundays in Sacramento are quiet, and most activity centers on church services. Like many other Costa Ricans, Cristiana and her family belong to the Roman Catholic church. Sacramento's small Catholic church perches on the mountainside not far from the Gonzáles-Hidalgo home. Everyone in Cristiana's family attends, as do many of their friends and neighbors.

The congregation listens intently as the village priest begins the Mass.

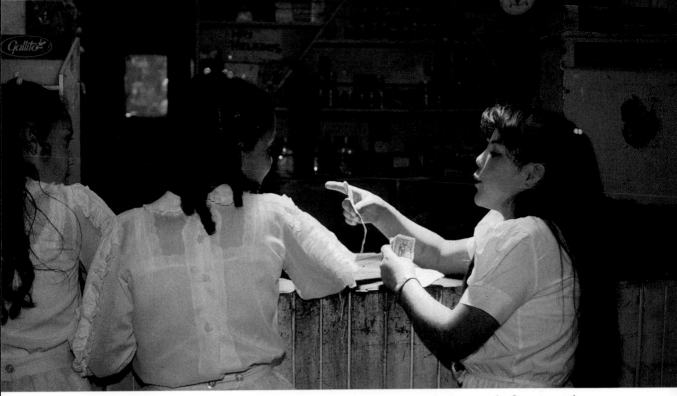

Between catechism class and Mass, the village store becomes a gathering spot for Sacramento's young people. Cristiana and her friends often walk there to buy a snack or to visit with other friends.

On Sunday mornings, Cristiana attends catechism, or religious instruction, class. The class lasts for two hours, after which she and her friends can play until church services start at 1:00 p.m. Sometimes, they run to Doña Teresita's store up the road to buy cookies and cold drinks. Today, they stand outside the store talking excitedly about tomorrow's school trip to the national park.

Doña Teresita packs the store shelves with groceries to keep up with her customers' needs.

A Class Field Trip to the National Park

A truck full of eager explorers rattles its way up the mountainside to the national park.

Once out of the truck, Cristiana and the other children scramble along the trail toward the volcano crater.

As part of their ecology studies, Cristiana's class has planned a trip to Braulio Carrillo National Park. This park, located atop the same mountain on which Sacramento sits, includes about 80,000 acres (32,000 ha) of rain forest. Cristiana is eager to explore the rain forest, where the trees grow so thick that they block the sky. She knows that many wild animals and over 850 different kinds of birds live in the forest. From her father, she has learned to identify many of them.

The class climbs into the back of a pickup truck for the short trip to the park. The truck winds up the mountain road, moving slowly because of the steep incline. When the truck reaches the park entrance, the explorers quickly pile out. They begin their tour by hiking about 1.2 miles (2 km) to the old crater of Barva Volcano. This volcano last erupted over a thousand years ago, and a lake with cold, clear water now fills its crater.

People can drink the cold, pure water that now fills the old crater of Barva Volcano.

Having completed the trek to the crater, Cristiana and her class pose victoriously before its sign.

Don Melvin gives the students a lesson on using a compass. He reminds them that a group of tourists lost its way in the dense forest near here several weeks before. The tourists wandered for two weeks before finding the trail again. Because they had studied the forest, they knew which wild plants, nuts, and berries to eat. Cristiana remembers seeing that story on television and thinks it would be frightening to be lost. She and Liliana stick close together.

After eating lunch on top of the volcano, the children play hide-and-seek, being careful not to go too far into the woods. When they tire of the game, they hike along a forest trail, stopping now and then to study the plant life. They finally turn onto the main trail and start back to the truck. After hiking in the dense forest, the trail seems very sunny. By the time they reach the truck, everyone is tired, and although the ride back to the school is bumpy, no one notices.

Above: The students listen carefully as Don Melvin explains how to use a compass. No one thinks getting lost sounds like much fun.
Left: Cristiana and a friend examine a huge fern growing along the path.